Parrot Talk

June Crebbin

Illustrated by Peter Kavanagh

CAMBRIDGE
UNIVERSITY PRESS

One morning at breakfast time, Tom said,
"Ben's a copycat."

"Cat," said Ben.

"See what I mean?" said Tom. "Why does
he copy everything I say?"

"Say," said Ben.

Dad laughed. "He's learning to talk," he said. "He hears what we say and then he tries to say it too."

"Just like a parrot," said Tom.

"Parrot," said Ben.

Everyone laughed. Ben grinned. He climbed down from his chair and lay on the floor to play with his cars.

There was a knock at the door. It was Etty, who lived across the road, and Sidney, her parrot. "Come in," said Mum. "We were just talking about parrots."

Etty put Sidney on the table.

"Hello Sidney," said Emma.

"Sidney is going to stay with us while Etty is
in hospital," said Mum.

"Oh good," said Tom. "I like Sidney."

"So do I," said Emma. "He says such funny things."

Etty smiled. "I hope he's good," she said. "Sometimes my sons were bad. They used to teach Sidney bad things."

But Tom and Emma loved to hear Sidney talk.
"I wonder if he'll say 'bad boy'," said Tom.
"Bad boy," said Ben, looking up.
"Oh no," said Dad. "Now we've got two talking parrots in the house!"

The next day, when Emma came home from school, Jess and Alice came too. They wanted to hear Sidney talk.

But Sidney didn't say a word. He just sat on his perch and hung his head.

Emma was disappointed.

"He can say 'Slobber-chops'," she said.

"And 'Droopy-drawers'!" said Tom.

But Sidney didn't say anything.

"Come on, Sidney," said Emma. "Say 'Slobber-chops'. Say 'Droopy-drawers'."

But Sidney didn't say anything. Every now and then he shifted along his perch, and Emma thought that he was going to talk.

But no matter how many words she tried,
Sidney said nothing.

"Bad boy," said Emma. "Bad boy." Even that
didn't work.

Alice and Jess went home.

In the hospital, Etty was beginning to get better. "How's my Sidney?" she would say as soon as Mum walked in to visit her.

"Fine," said Mum. "He's fine."

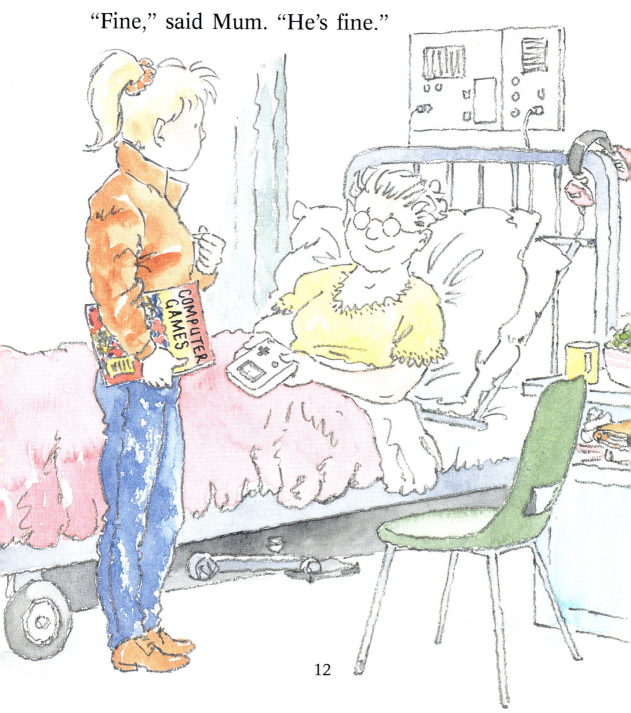

But still, Mum was worried that he wasn't talking. Usually, he was such a chatterbox. She thought he might be ill.

So she took him to the vet.

The vet looked at Sidney and listened to Mum.
Then the vet said, "Perhaps he's missing home.
Sometimes parrots aren't very happy in a strange
place. Perhaps he's missing his peace and quiet."

"Oh dear," said Mum. "He doesn't get much
of that in our house!"

"There's nothing to worry about," said the vet.
"He's fine."

Sometimes, in the afternoons when the house was quiet, Mum thought that she heard voices in the living-room. But every time she went to have a look, there was Ben "brum-brumming" with his cars quietly on the floor, and there was Sidney in his cage.

But Sidney wasn't saying anything.

Everyone tried to get Sidney to talk. Dad kept
saying, "Who's a pretty boy then?"

Tom and Emma kept trying all of Sidney's
favourite sayings. They said, "Slobber-chops"
and "Droopy-drawers" and "Give us a kiss."

But Sidney said nothing.

One afternoon, Mum and Ben went to Tom and
Emma's school. There was a book sale in the hall.
Mum looked at the books with Ben.

Then Mum looked at the books on her own, and
Ben played with another little boy. They chased
each other round and round the hall. Then they
sat on some steps and chattered. Ben had become
a proper little chatterbox.

Tom and Emma met Mum in the hall after school. Emma's teacher was there too, choosing some books.

When it was time to go, Mum collected Tom and Emma and they all looked for Ben. He was chasing his new friend round the hall again.

"Time to go," called Mum, but Ben didn't want to go. When Mum caught him he tried to get free. At that moment, Emma's teacher came up to say hello.

"Is this Ben?" she said. "I've heard a lot about you."

"Slobber-chops," said Ben.
The teacher's mouth dropped open.
"Pardon," she said.
"Droopy-drawers," said Ben.

"Time to go," said Mum firmly. She smiled at
the teacher. "Sorry," she said. "Goodbye."
  "Goodbye," said the teacher.

"Bad boy," said Ben, as they set off. "Bad boy."

"Yes, you are," said Mum. "And I know who's been talking to you."

"Sidney!" cried Tom and Emma.

Ben grinned. "Give us a kiss," he said.